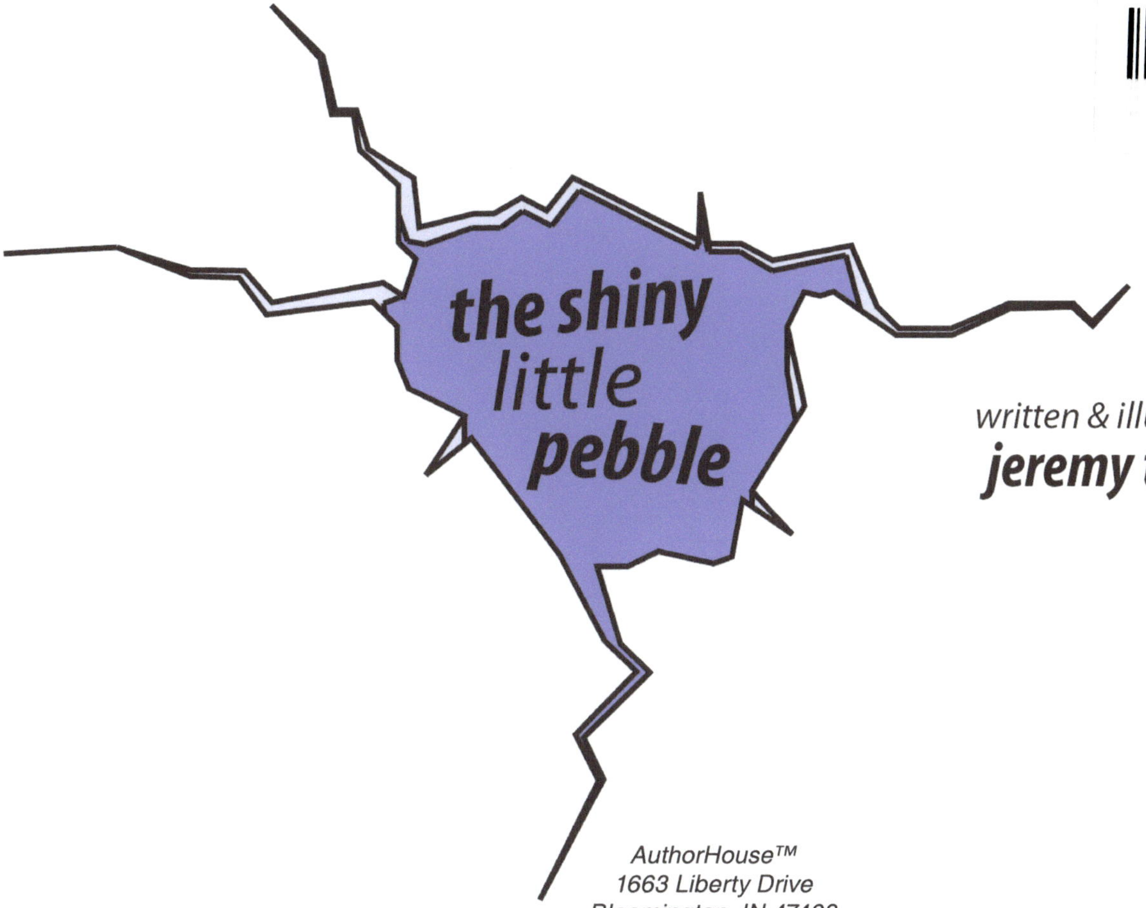

the shiny little pebble

written & illustrated by
jeremy t white

AuthorHouse™
1663 Liberty Drive
Bloomington, IN 47403
www.authorhouse.com
Phone: 1-800-839-8640

First published by AuthorHouse 5/31/2011

ISBN: 978-1-4634-0496-3
Library of Congress Control Number: 2011907914

Printed in the United States of America
This book is printed on acid-free paper.

authorHOUSE®

Somewhere under the icy blanket
of Cozy River,

lived a shiny little pebble
as quiet as he could be.

1

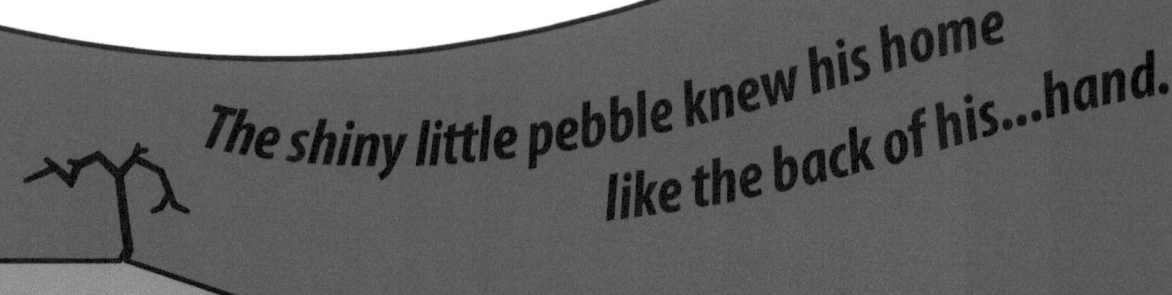

The shiny little pebble knew his home like the back of his...hand.

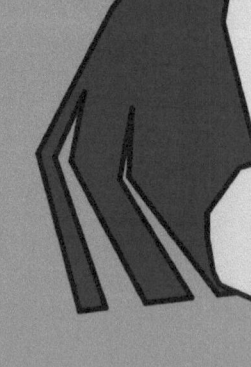

After all, he had been there since forever fell asleep...

...and time woke up!

2

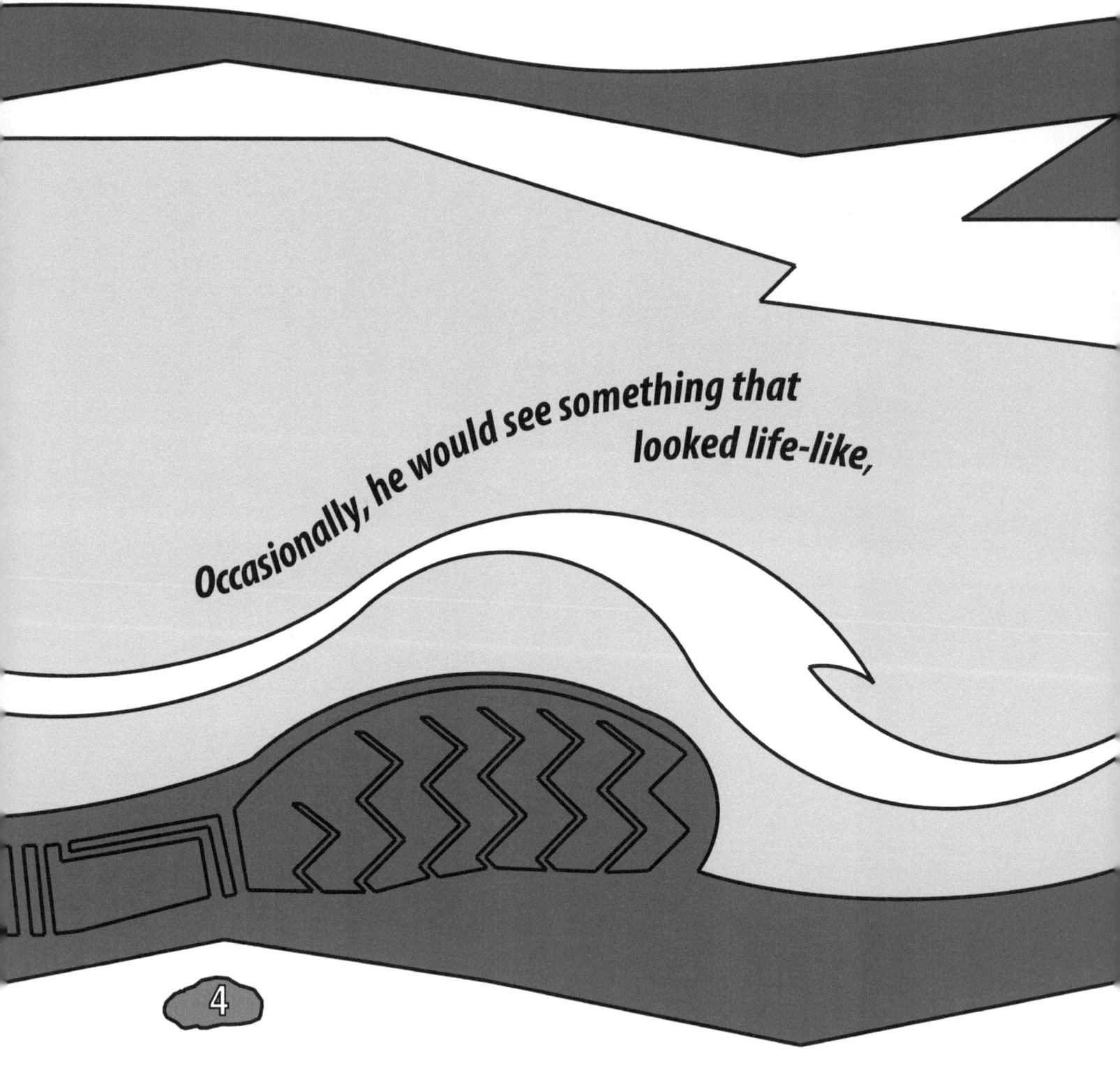

Occasionally, he would see something that looked life-like,

but usually it was just
a piece of torn-up trash tossed in the river.

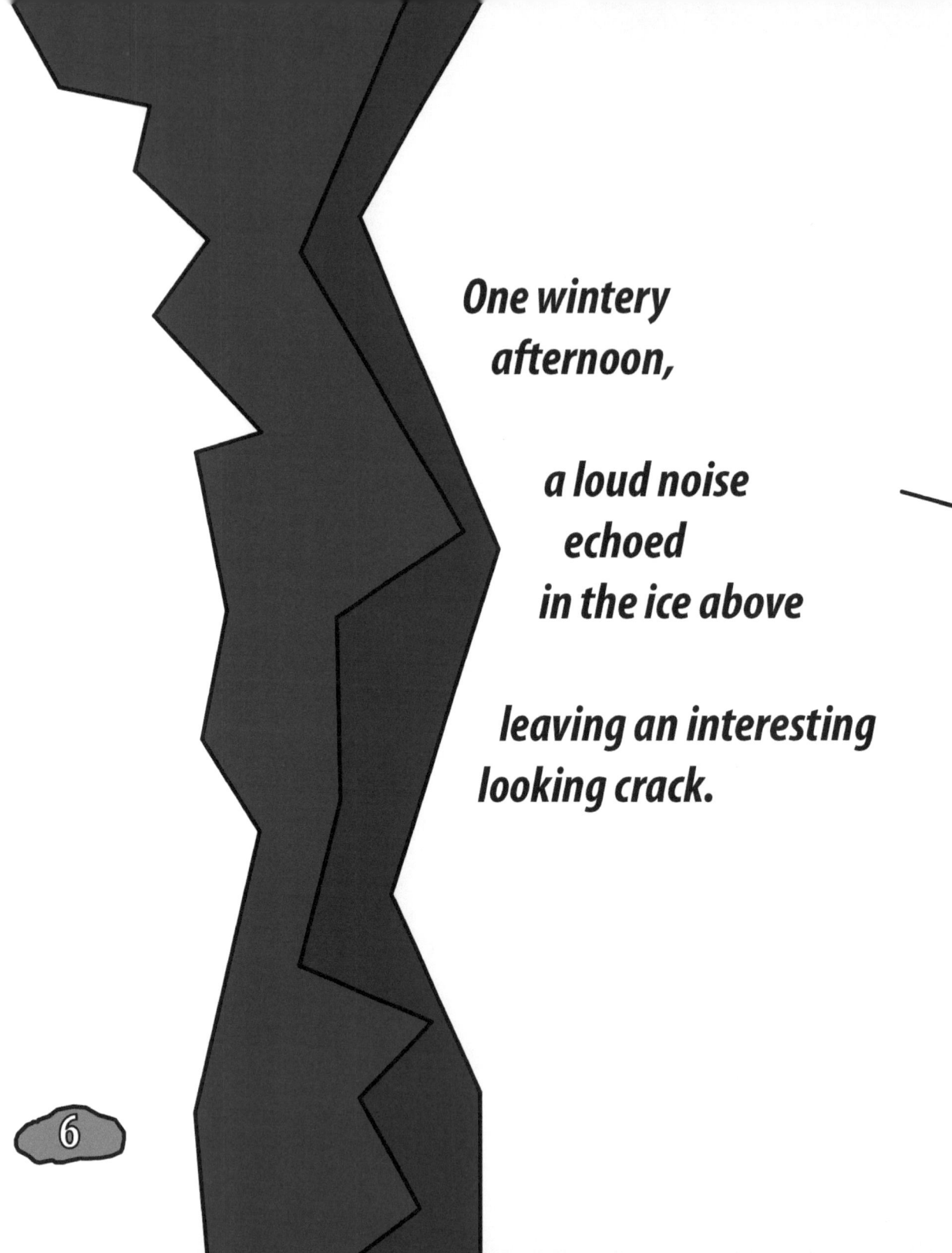

One wintery
afternoon,

a loud noise
echoed
in the ice above

leaving an interesting
looking crack.

6

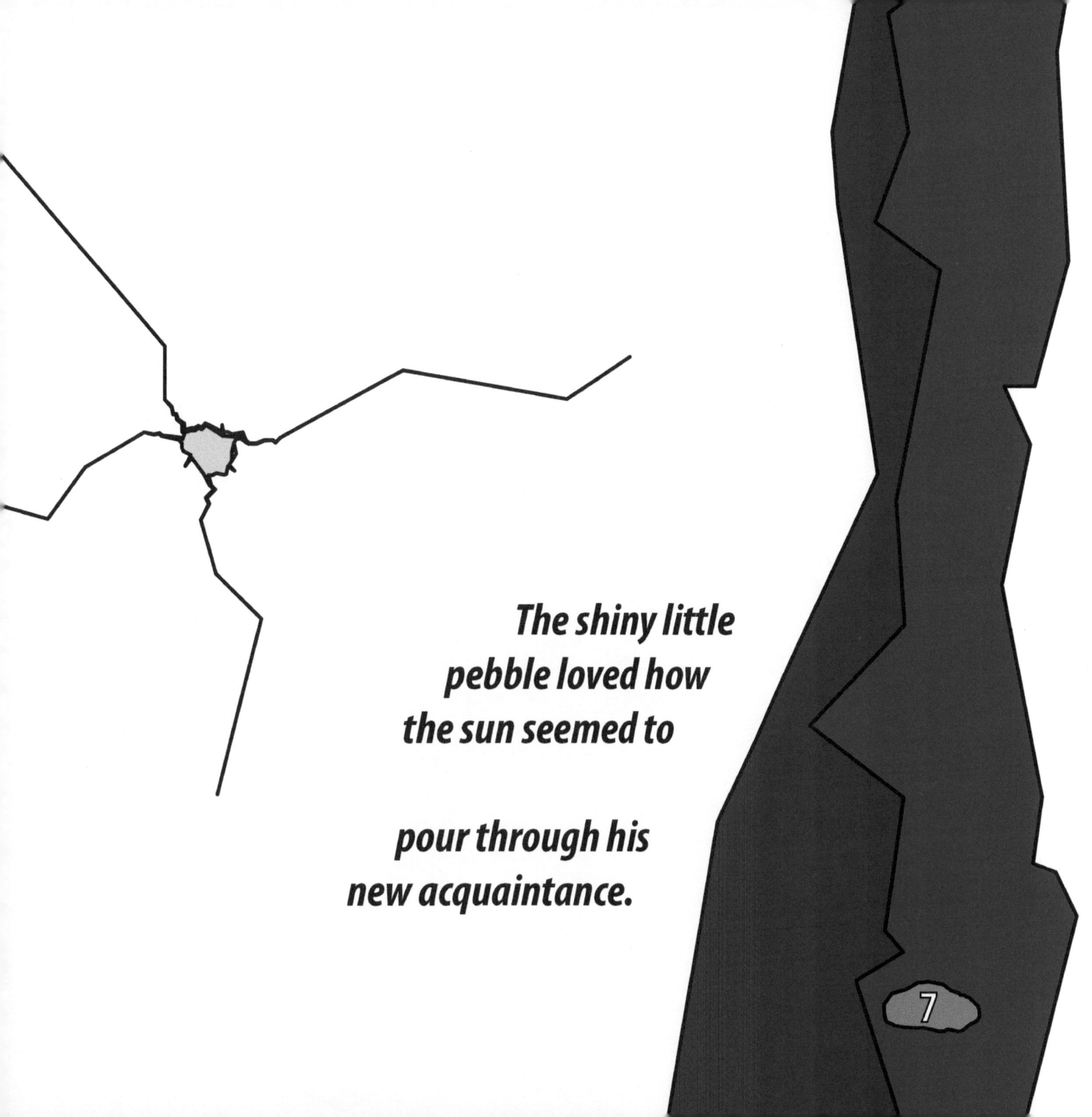

The shiny little pebble loved how the sun seemed to

pour through his new acquaintance.

7

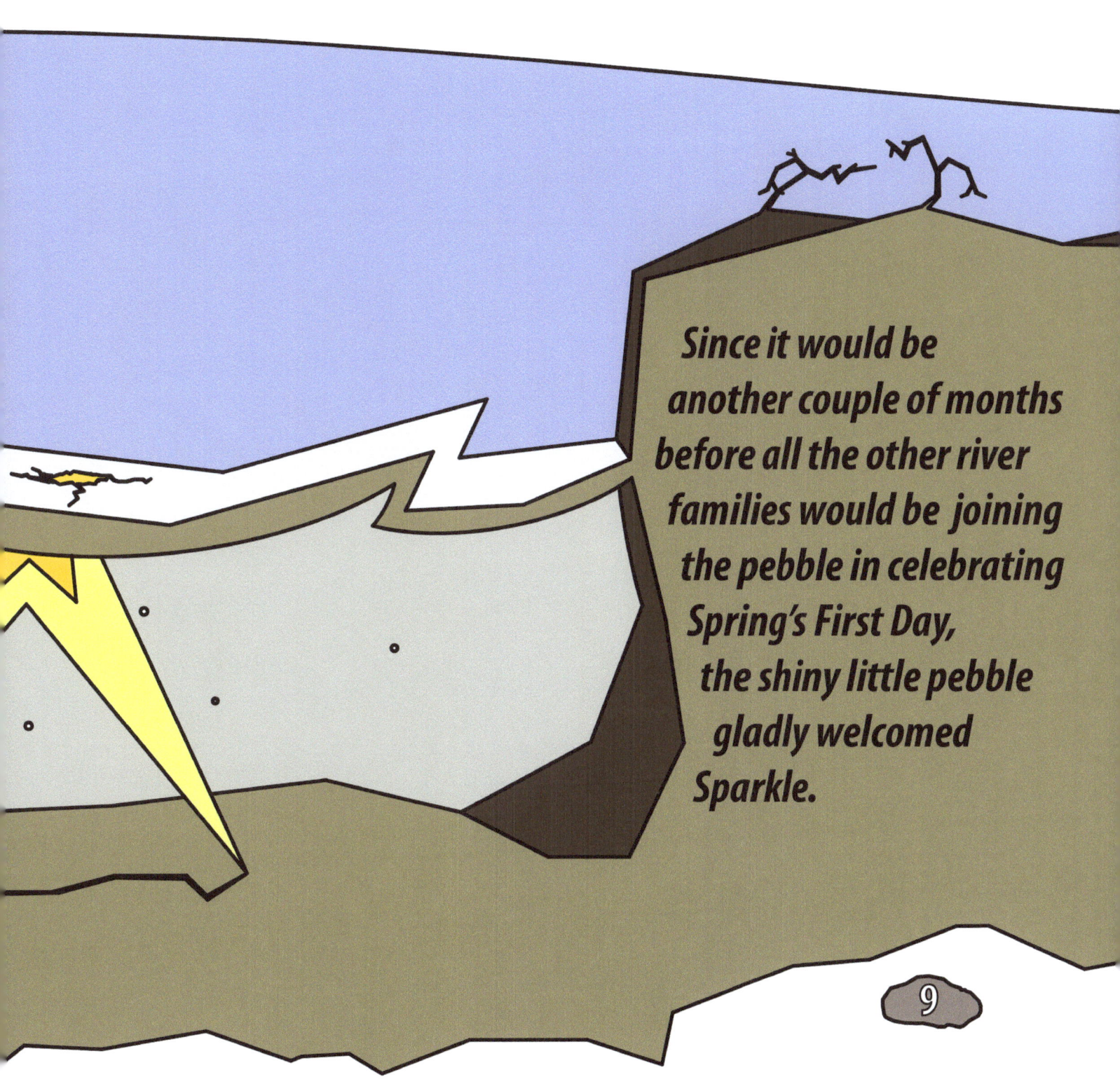

Since it would be another couple of months before all the other river families would be joining the pebble in celebrating Spring's First Day, the shiny little pebble gladly welcomed Sparkle.

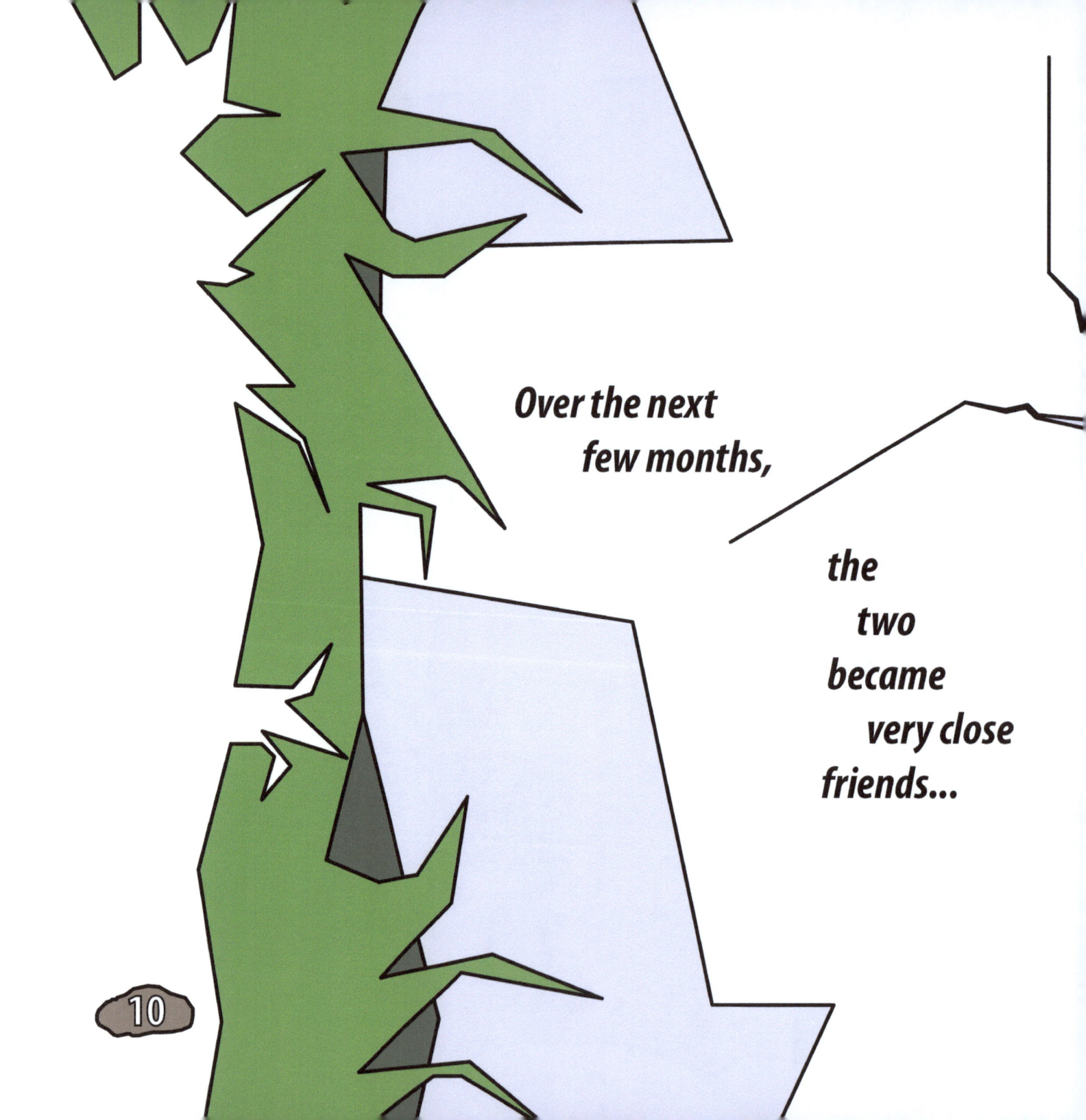

Over the next few months, the two became very close friends...

10

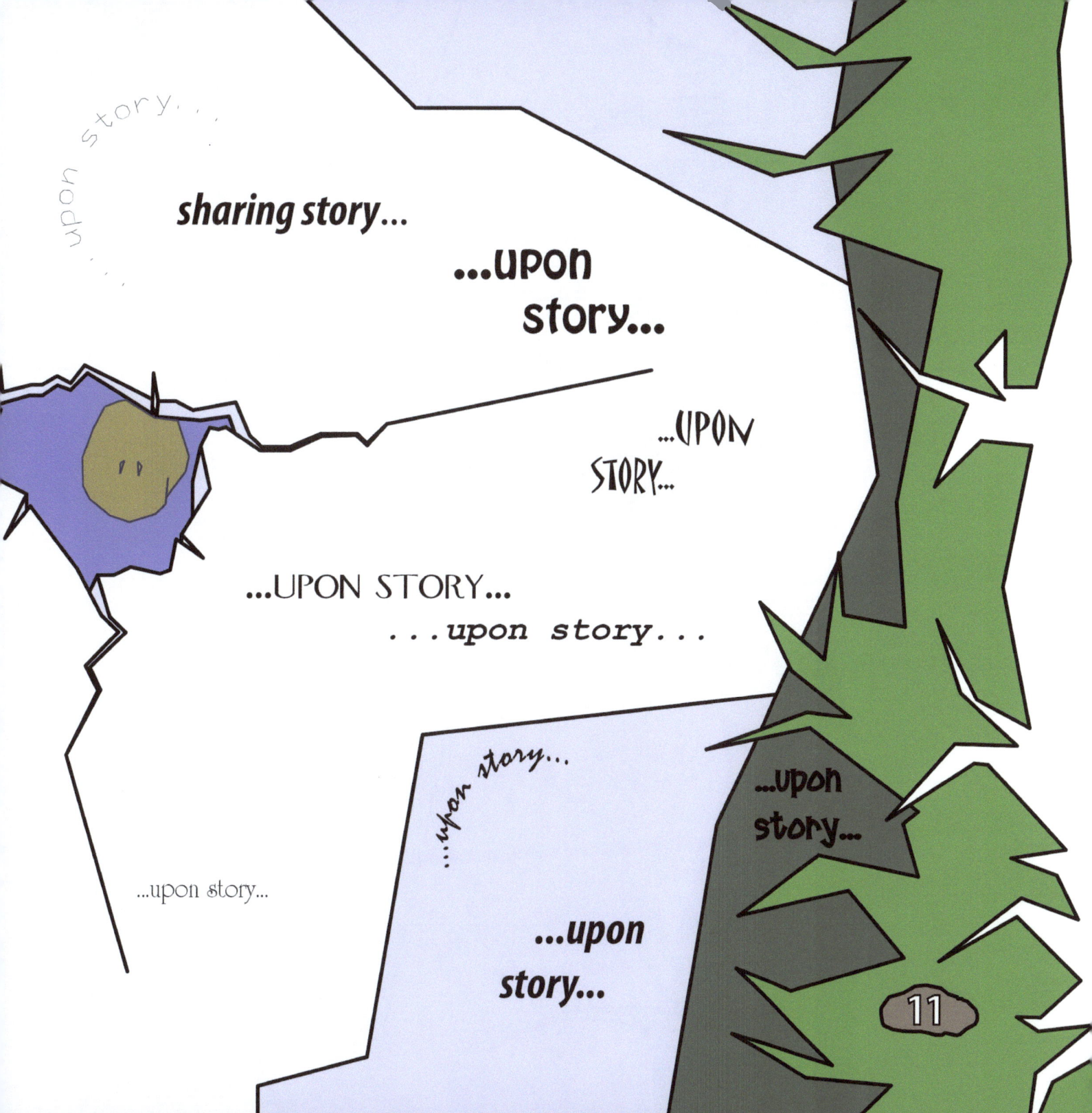

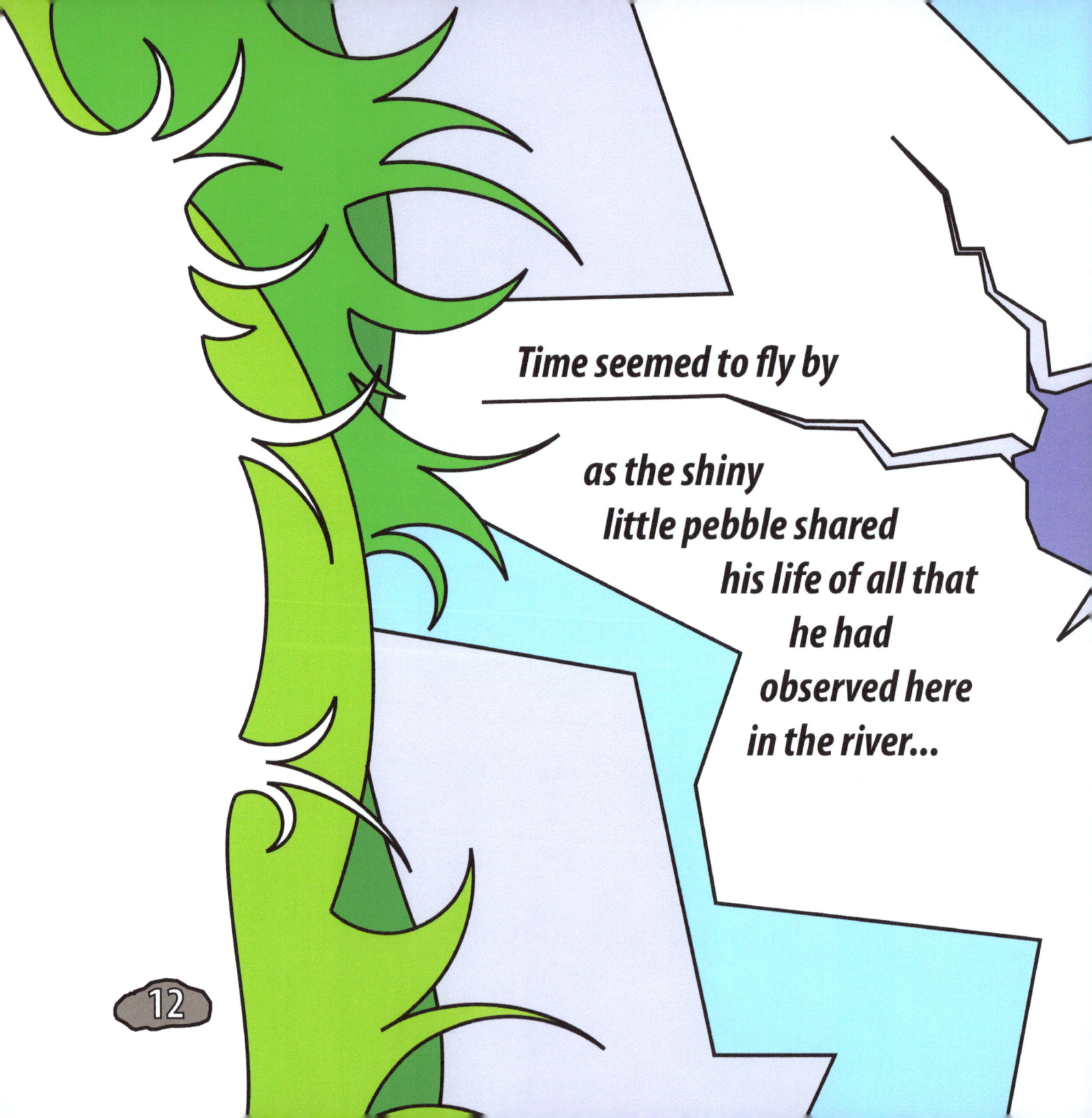

Time seemed to fly by

as the shiny
little pebble shared
his life of all that
he had
observed here
in the river...

12

...Faster than you can say Sassafras Splash, Spring had finally sprung!

...the shiny little pebble had one thing on his mind...finding Sparkle. He couldn't wait to celebrate Spring's First Day & introduce all the river families to his new friend Sparkle!

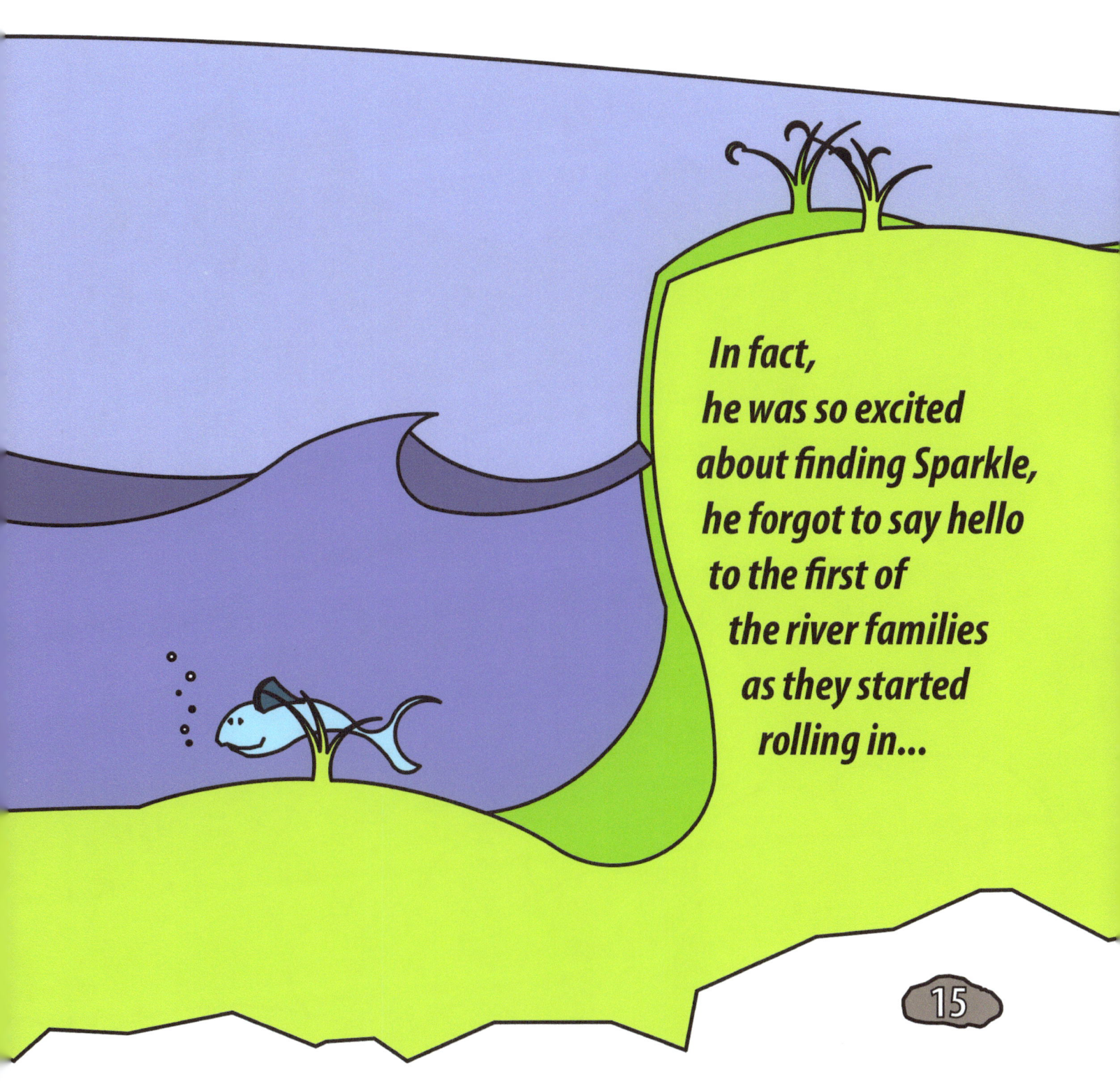

In fact,
he was so excited
about finding Sparkle,
he forgot to say hello
to the first of
the river families
as they started
rolling in...

15

...Sparkle was no where to be found.

Now there would be no one
he could celebrate
Spring's First Day with...

18

...except for that family of daisies that had just popped up for the celebration.

If they couldn't cheer him up...no one could...

19

...and what about all those new budding plants...but...

"What would they see in a little pebble like me?"

The shiny little pebble knew that Sparkle would love nothing more than for him to enjoy himself celebrating the grand opening of Spring...

21

To his surprise,
the shiny little pebble
was received
with open arms
from everyone.

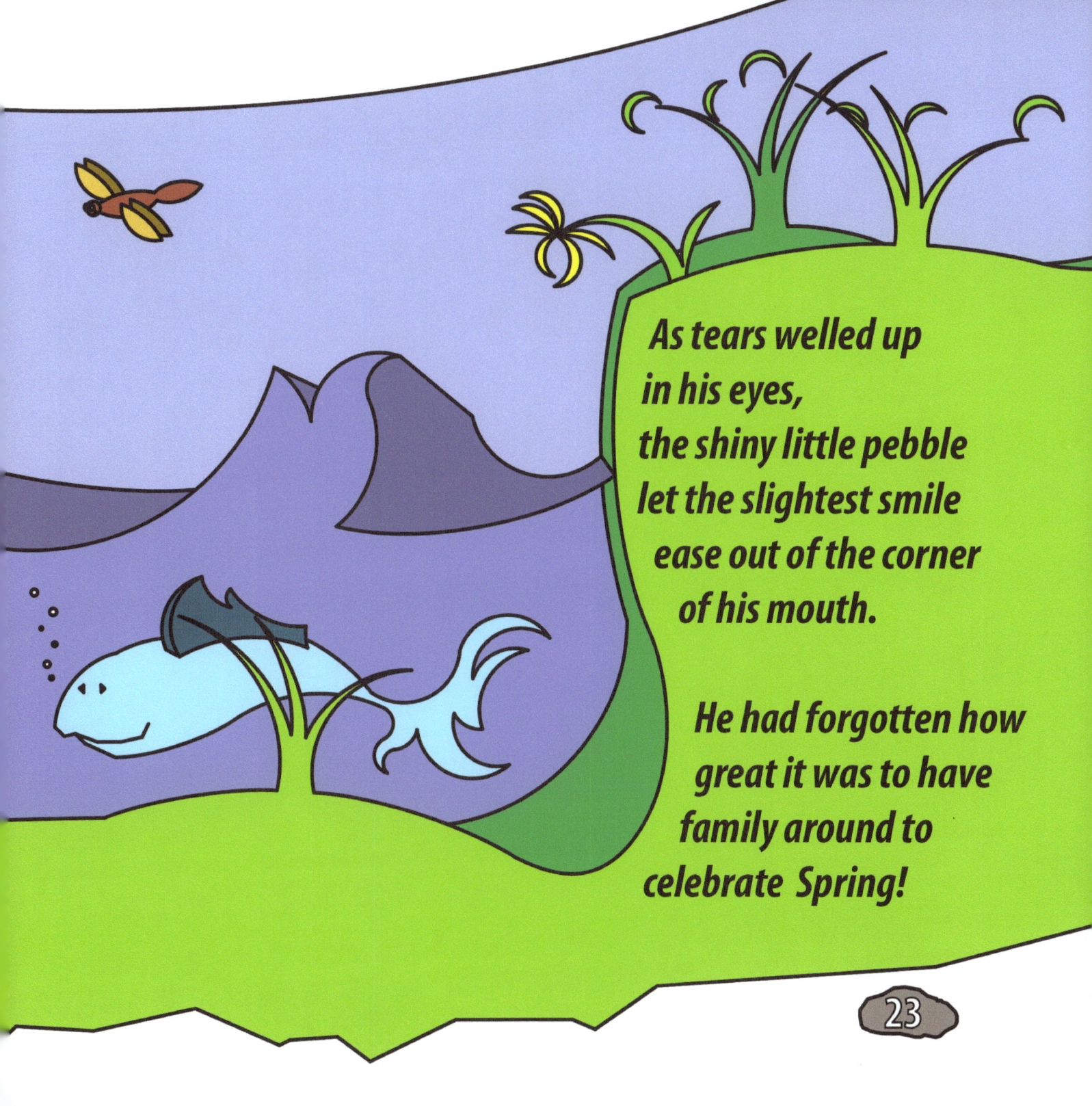

As tears welled up
in his eyes,
the shiny little pebble
let the slightest smile
ease out of the corner
of his mouth.

He had forgotten how
great it was to have
family around to
celebrate Spring!

So, after a long day of
celebrating with friends & family,
the shiny
little pebble
snuggled into his old bed
of silt and sand
for a good
night sleep.

As his eyes slowly
    pulled the curtains to Spring's First Day,
        the shiny little pebble was already waiting...

...Summer's Hottest Day was just around the corner!